First published in Great Britain in 1983 by
Macmillan Publishers Limited under the title
Speed Sports

This edition published in 1989 by
Treasure Press
Michelin House
81 Fulham Road
London SW3 6RB

ISBN 1 85051 367 8

Produced by Mandarin Offset
Printed and bound in Hong Kong

Editor: Miranda Smith
Designer: Julian Holland
Picture Researcher: Stella Martin
Photo Credits: All Sport Photographic 2-3, 4-5, 6-7, 10, 11,
14, 15, 20-1, 34-5, 35, 38, 40, 44, 61, 63 below, 69 below,
72, 72-3, 74, 75 above and below, 77 above and below; 78,
86-7, 88-9, 95; Animal Photography 42-3; Jonathan Ashman 59;
Australian Information Service 13 below, 91; BBC Hulton
Picture Library 12 right, 16 left, 46 below, 54, 63 above,
66 above, 69 above, 90; Diana Burnett 53, 57, 58;
J. Allan Cash 23 above, 80 below, 92; Martin Christidis 64-5;
Gerry Cranham 18, 23 below, 45, 47, 48-9, 58-9; Mary Evans
Picture Library Endpapers, 6, 16 right, 20, 24 above and below,
36, 67 above and below, 68, 70, 76; Ian Gooch 28-9 above,
Ian Griffiths 85; Alan Hutchison Library 56-7; Colin
Jarman 81, 82, 83, 93; Kobal Collection 71; Mansell
Collection 12 left; Popperfoto 13 above, 63 middle; Steve
Rees 22; Rex Features 80 above; Scala/Firenze 28-9 below,
30-1; Mark Shearman 8, 9, 10-11, 16-17; Nigel Snowdon 51,
55 below, 56, 89, 94; Spectrum 19; Syndication International
90-1; Vision International 26-7; Peter Newark's Western
Americana 66 below; ZEFA 25, 32-3, 37, 39, 40-1, 43, 46 above,
50, 52-3, 55 above, 60, 60-1, 78-9, 84, 92-3
Cover picture: All Sport Photographic
Artwork: Allan Nutbrown 7, 36-7

THE FASTEST Sports IN THE WORLD

TREASURE PRESS

Contents

A race against the clock! A competitor in the World White Water Canoeing Championships paddles desperately through rough water. All sorts of obstacles must be avoided in order to secure a fast time.

Introduction

The quest of men and women for speed goes back almost to the beginning of recorded time. In ancient mythology the gods themselves were famed for their fleetness of foot. Hermes, the messenger of the gods, was said by the Greeks to have had wings on his heels in order to travel faster. The Nordic god, Thor, was said to cause the noise of thunder by rumbling across the heavens at great speed in an enormous chariot!

In history, too, the fastest messengers became heroes. Sometimes their feats were exaggerated until they became legends, as in the story of the Greek soldier who, in 490 BC, was reported to have run the 40 kilometres from the site of the battle of Marathon to Athens, bearing the news of the Greek victory over the Persians.

Today people can move at speeds which once would have been considered fantastic. They can run for short distances at a rate of 40 kilometres an hour, and hurtle through space in rockets a thousand times faster. They are striving constantly to attain greater speeds on land, in the water and in the air.

In order to do this, people have, over the centuries, raced against each other on foot, on the backs of animals and in many different kinds of vehicles. They have taken great risks, pushing their bodies, their mounts and their machines to the limit.

It is no coincidence that the motto of the greatest of all sporting occasions, the Olympic Games, is 'swifter, higher, stronger'. In all of the various sports in which they have taken part, athletes and machines have travelled at ever-increasing rates. In the process they have provided the world with some of its most thrilling moments, and continue to do so to this day.

Completely motionless after a frantic burst of activity, the ski-jumper soars through the air. His body leans forward, arms by the sides and skis close together. To achieve this posture, the jumper must leave the in-run at speed.

The Speed of Man

Walking

Walking really became recognized as a sport in the 19th century, thanks mainly to the efforts of a Scot, R.B. Allardice, better known as 'Captain Barclay'. In 1809, he walked 1,000 miles (1,609 kilometres) in 1,000 hours. Long-distance walking events became the rage, and vast sums of money were wagered on them. Captain Barclay became a trainer of prize-fighters, making the pugilists in his care walk long distances every day.

Walking races have continued to be a popular sport with both athletes and spectators. In modern races the distances covered range from three to 100 kilometres. The main distances in international events are 20 and 50 kilometres. It is very difficult to decide when a competitor has infringed the rules in a walking event, and the judging is a very complicated affair.

Above: In modern walking events, like the 1974 European championships shown here, the feet of the walkers must keep unbroken contact with the ground. This insistence on 'toe-and-heel' contact is strictly observed and failure can lead to disqualification.

Left: 'Pedestrianism', as the sport was known, was very popular towards the end of the 19th century. Six-day events, like the one shown on the left, drew large crowds to watch professional walkers compete in 'go-as-you-please' indoor races in the USA. In these events walkers could remain on the track as long as they wanted, and then rest. The winner was the one who had covered the greatest distance on the circular track at the end of the six days.

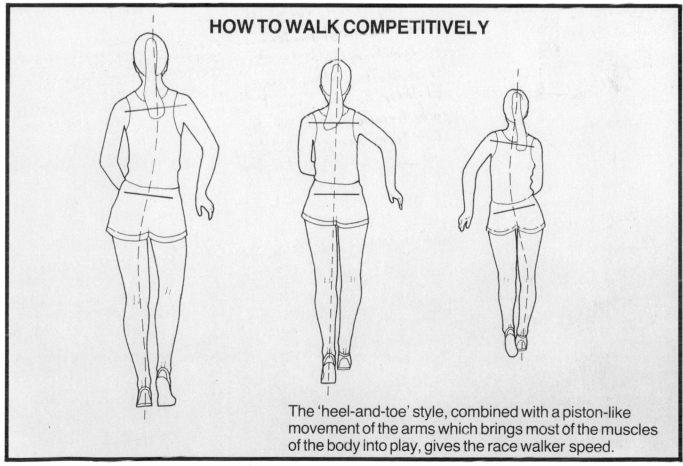

HOW TO WALK COMPETITIVELY

The 'heel-and-toe' style, combined with a piston-like movement of the arms which brings most of the muscles of the body into play, gives the race walker speed.

Sprinting

Men and women probably first realized the importance of being able to run quickly over short distances in prehistoric times. The first hunters often had to turn and flee from the wild beasts they had been tracking. Those who survived would then encourage their children to race against each other, and so build up speed in case they too should have to run for their lives one day.

From these primitive beginnings grew great sporting events like the Olympic Games of the ancient Greeks. To this day sprinting has been held to be very important at all athletics tournaments. Sprinters are the fastest and perhaps the most exciting of all runners.

At modern meetings, 'sprint' is the name given to every race up to and including the 400 metres. In all international competitions these events consist of the 100 metres, 200 metres and 400 metres races. A good sprinter can run at speeds of up to 40 kilometres an hour.

Below: Sprint events are over in such a short time that everything depends upon getting a good start. At first, sprinters started from an upright stance at a shout of 'Go', a drum-beat or the drop of a white handkerchief. Then, in 1888, an American athlete, Charles Sherrill – who later became a general – invented the crouch start. Other developments included the use of a pistol to get runners away even more quickly, and starting-blocks which gave added thrust at the beginning of a sprint.

Relay

One of the earliest and most effective ways of carrying messages for long distances was by positioning runners along an agreed route, so that a fresh man was always ready to take over from an exhausted one.

After the first contest between the universities of Oxford and Cambridge, in 1864, athletics developed into a team sport. Coaches and trainers siezed upon the relay system as a way of building up club spirit and emphasizing the elements of co-operation in running.

Over the years experiments were made with a number of different distances and methods of relay running. These included the so-called 'shuttle' system in which one runner ran the normal direction round the track and then touched the second man in the team, who ran back in the direction from which the first man had come, and so on. Eventually, however, the system which was adopted consisted of four-men teams, each runner going round the track the same way.

In international competitions there are nine main forms of relay race, each containing a team of four runners. For men, the shortest distance is one in which each athlete runs 100 metres (4 x 100 metres), and the longest is one in which each man runs 1,500 metres (4 x 1,500 metres).

The longest distance on a track for women is 4 x 800 metres. A baton must be passed from hand to hand in a 20 metre take-over area. Each runner must hold the baton throughout his or her 'leg' of the race, and must stop to retrieve it if it is dropped. Passing the baton correctly is a tricky business and requires a great deal of practice.

Hurdling

A race which consisted of sprinting over a course and at the same time jumping over a number of low obstacles was first reported at an athletics meeting in England in the year 1850. Fourteen years later it was included in the Oxford University sports. The race took place over a distance of 120 yards (109 metres) and the obstacles consisted of a number of sheep hurdles. The event took its name from the sheep hurdles.

These first hurdles were a little over a metre in height. Athletes used a number of different styles with which to clear them. In 1886, a student at Oxford University devised a method of leaping over the hurdles with the leading leg extended and straight. In this way, the speed for the distance was increased considerably, and has been improving ever since.

In international competitions today hurdle races take place over distances of 110 metres and 400 metres for men, and 100 metres for women. Hurdles are also included among other obstacles, like water jumps, in the steeplechase event of 3,000 metres.

Above: This is the steeple-chase event in the Moscow Olympics in 1980. The runners had to go round the track twice and clear 28 hurdles and seven water jumps in the process.

Left: Fanny Blankers-Koen of Holland wins the 80 metres hurdles event at the 1948 Olympics in London. She may have been the greatest of all women athletes. Although she was 30 years old, she won four gold medals at these games.

Right: Edwin Moses of the USA broke the world record while winning the 400 metres hurdles at the Montreal Olympics in 1976. His time of 47.64 seconds saw him win by over a second.

Personalities

In the 1908 Olympics 400-metres final, there was only one competitor. The first attempt to run the final had been declared 'no race' because, it was claimed, the three Americans in the race had impeded the lone Briton, Wyndham Halswell. Officials broke the tape before any of the runners could reach it, so that the final could not be completed. They ordered the race to be re-run. The three Americans refused to compete, saying that they had done nothing wrong. In the end, Halswell ran in the second final by himself before an enthusiastic crowd at the White City Stadium in London. Two British sprinters, Harold Abrahams and Eric Liddell, often ran against each other. It was thought that either could win the 100 metres sprint at the 1924 Paris Olympics. But when Liddell, a devout Christian, heard that the heats of the race were to be run on a Sunday, he refused to compete. Harold Abrahams went on to win the gold medal. Liddell than entered the 400 metres instead and won the race, although it was an event he knew little about. He then gave up athletics and went to China as a missionary.

An American negro called Jesse Owens was one of the greatest athletes who ever lived. In one 45-minute period in 1935, he broke or equalled six world records. He then went on to the 1936 Olympic Games in Berlin and won gold medals in the 100 and 200 metres, the long jump and the 4 x 100 metres relay. Owens never went on to the heights expected of him as an athlete. During the Great Depression of the 1930s there was little work for a black man in the USA. Owens turned professional at the age of 23, and spent his time in running against horses and similar stunts.

In the heats of the 100 metres sprint at the 1924 Olympics, which were held in Paris, the Briton Harold Abrahams equalled the world record of 10.6 seconds.

Jesse Owens is pictured here at the start of the 200 metres final in the 1936 Olympics, which he won in 20.7 seconds. The Olympics were held in Berlin.

The first sub four-minute mile (1.6 kilometres) was run at the Iffley Road track, Oxford, on 6 May, 1954. Roger Bannister, seen above running behind one of his pace-makers, Chris Brasher, and in front of another, Christopher Chataway, won the race in 3 minutes 59.4 seconds. Bannister was knighted in 1975. Brasher won a gold medal in the 1956 Olympics. Once Bannister had broken the 4-minute barrier other athletes followed him, running the mile even faster. In the same year, John Landy of Australia broke Bannister's mile record but was defeated by the Briton in the Commonwealth Games mile race in the time of 3 minutes 58.8 seconds.

Right: Herb Elliott, the Australian, seen here in a 4 x 1 mile medley relay, won the Olympic 1500 metres in 1960 by a distance of 20 metres. In his entire career he never lost over the 1,500 metres or 1 mile distances.

Running

Middle-distance events are those run over 800 and 1,500 metres, and the 3,000 metres steeplechase. The long-distances races are the 5,000 metres, the 10,000 metres and the marathon. Some athletes have shown great versatility, being able to perform well over different distances.

Emile Zatopek, an officer in the Czechoslovakian Army, won gold medals in the 1952 Olympics at 5,000 and 10,000 metres. He then decided to enter the marathon. He had never run in one and knew so little about the event that while he was competing in it he had to ask the other runners if he was going fast enough! In fact he went fast enough to win the race and a third gold medal.

Another great middle- and long-distance runner was Paavo Nurmi, 'the Flying Finn'. Between 1921 and 1931 he won 12 Olympic medals and broke world records at 1,500, 5,000 and 10,000 metres, 1 miles, 3 miles, 6 miles and 10 miles.

Right: Two of the greatest runners of the moment are the Britons Sebastian Coe and Steve Ovett. Between 1979 and 1981, Coe broke the world mile record three times, and Ovett did so twice. In the 1980 Moscow Olympics, Ovett won the 800 metres, and Coe was second. In the 1,500 metres Coe came first; Ovett was third.

Below: Another fine runner over many different distances in the 1970s and 1980s was the Ethiopian Miruts Yifter, seen here second in the field. He was renowned for his ability to change pace and could move through a crowded field at great speed. This gained him the nickname of 'Yifter the Shifter'.

Marathon

As a matter of tradition, the marathon is the long-distance event which ends major athletics tournaments as a grand climax. At such meetings the marathon usually starts in the stadium, is held over a looping course in the streets outside, and then finishes at the stadium again. A famous marathon route at the 1908 London Olympics was 42,195 metres. It was that long because that was the distance between Windsor Castle and the White City Stadium, the route of the race. This is now recognized as the standard distance for the event.

The race is a gruelling and exhausting one, lasting over two hours. Many runners fail to complete the course. One of the greatest of all marathon runners was the Ethiopian Abebe Bikila, who won two successive Olympic marathons in record times in 1960 and 1964. In the first event he covered the route running in his bare feet.

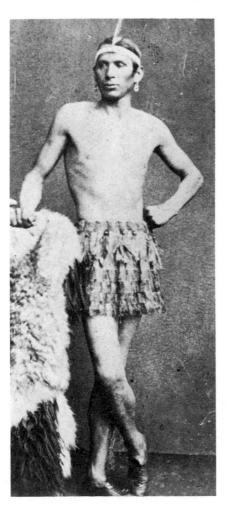

Left: Deerfoot, who ran as 'The Seneca Indian', was one of a number of Indians who did well at distance running.

Below: Dorando Pietri of Italy is being helped to the tape in the 1908 Olympic marathon. He was too exhausted to finish on his own, and was disqualified.

Marathon races became amazingly popular during the 1970s. Thousands of men and women enter these long-distance races all over the world. Most of them do not expect to win, but are content if they are able to complete the course. The four best-known of the marathons are the two held in the USA, in New York and Boston, the London one in Great Britain, and the Japanese Fukuoka marathon.

The first three are open to all athletes, but the Japanese race allows only 150 runners or so to enter. The best three marathon racers from each country are invited to compete, as long as they complete a course in 2 hours 2 minutes 14 seconds or less.

Above: The start of the New York marathon in 1981. A vast crowd of runners started the course. The race was won by Alberto Salazar. His time of 2 hours 3 minutes was claimed as a world record. However, marathon courses vary so much from place to place that it is difficult to compare them. The USA is usually recognized as the home of the best marathon runners. In 1980, it had 37 runners who could complete a marathon in under 2 hours 2 minutes 16 seconds.

Children Racing

Children are encouraged to take part in athletics events from quite a young age by the national athletics bodies of most nations. Children of seven to nine often compete in sprint events, and from the age of about eleven there are national standards for each age group. If a boy or girl can produce a suitable time for a particular event he or she will be awarded a badge or certificate.

In Great Britain older boys and girls are divided into Youths (15 to 17 years) and Juniors (17 to 19 years) by the Amateur Athletics Association, which governs the sport. This means that young people do not strain themselves too much by competing outside their own age-group.

Many famous athletes were first noticed as promising schoolchildren in various events and were then given coaching to improve their natural ability – for example, in Britain, Sebastian Coe and Steve Ovett. Unfortunately, not all promising young runners keep on with their athletics.

Children can compete in events which range from novelty races in the primary school (below), to full-scale cross-country competitions (right).

The first cross-country races took the form of 'hare and hounds' events. Two runners are chosen to be the 'hares' and are given pouches of turn up waste-paper to carry. They are then allowed to set off before the other runners, the 'hounds'. The first two runners have to lay a trail of paper for the main body of runners to follow. The 'hounds' then have to catch up with the 'hares'. If they have time the 'hares' try to lay false trails in an attempt to put off the other runners and get away.

Racing Animals

After people began to keep domesticated animals they used them for a variety of purposes – carrying, hunting and as a source of food. Then they discovered that if they raced the faster ones against each other for sport, the animals could provide good entertainment.

Among the first animals to be used in this fashion were the coursing dogs of the ancient Egyptians. These were the fast-moving Salukis, which were used to chase wild animals while their owners looked on. Horses, too, were raced against each other. The Romans used teams of them to pull chariots in competitions in their arenas. At the first Olympic Games the results of events were sent back to the homelands of the competitors by racing pigeons. Before long these pigeons were being raced against one another and today pigeon-racing is a very popular sport.

Hundreds of years later dog-sled races became popular in Canada and Alaska after the first white trappers had competed against the local Eskimos.

Above: For a time greyhound racing was considered immoral, because the dogs chased and killed live rabbits. Then, in 1919, an American called Owen Smith invented a mechanical hare for the dogs to pursue. This made greyhound racing respectable.

Left: Races between riders on horses and bicycles became popular briefly in the 1890s. This picture shows Miss Nelly of the USA, on horseback, racing in Munich against a German cyclist, Amanda Loscuke. In the best-known of such races, John Prince, a cyclist, was defeated by 46 seconds by a horse and rider over a 20-mile (32 kilometre) course in Florida.

As well as the more orthodox methods of animal racing, there have also been more unusual competitions. In the 1920s there were even races between greyhounds ridden by monkeys. These were soon banned as being too cruel. On the island of Madura in the Dutch East Indies (now Indonesia) races between bulls were very popular at this time. The government bred the animals on a special farm and kept them just for racing.

Perhaps the most unusual of all animal competitions was the one known as the 'Frog Olympics', held in Florida in 1937. The climax of the competition was a leaping contest involving 100 frogs. It was won by Gas House Gus with a leap of over six metres. For a time such competitions became popular, but they fell out of favour when it was discovered that unscrupulous owners were rooting their opponents' frogs to the ground, by feeding them with handfuls of lead shot before the contests were due to start.

The origins of horse-racing probably stretch back over thousands of years. By the Middle Ages horse-races were quite common in Europe. The first public race course was opened at Smithfield, in London, in 1170. Riders competed for glory, not prizes, but in 1540 riders and their mounts were competing for a silver ball at the Chester Fair. Some years later a silversmith making the silver ball for the winner failed with his first and second attempts, before completing a satisfactory prize. As there were two balls left after the winner had received his, the remaining ones were given to the riders of the next two horses in the race. This is how the custom of giving first, second and third prizes originated.

At the beginning of the 19th century it was decided to separate the best racehorses into a special group called thoroughbreds. Any horse which could trace its ancestry to one of three fine horses known to be descended from Arabian stock was declared to be a thoroughbred.

Today horse-races are held all over the world, like this one taking place in the West Indies. Races usually take place on an oval track, and the traditional unit of measurement used is the one known as the 'furlong'. The jockeys wear colourful blouses known as 'silks', each horse owner having his own colours.

Some races take place over obstacles known as 'jumps', and others are held on the 'flat'. Flat race jockeys usually have to weigh under 115 pounds (52 kilos), but those riding over the jumps may weigh more. A horse which is thought to have a good chance of winning a race may be 'handicapped' by being made to carry a heavier weight than the other horses.

Above: Harness racing is very popular in the USA. Contests are held on a track between horses pulling two-wheeled lightweight carts, each with a driver. The horses are bred for this event. When they run they lift their forelegs and their opposite hind legs at the same time. This gives them a very distinctive gait.

Right: Shergar wins the 1981 Derby at Epsom in Surrey. The Derby is the best-known of all English flat races. Run over a distance of 1 ½ miles (2,400 metres), it is open to three-year-old colts and fillies. It was first run on Epsom Downs in 1780. It was named after its founder, the 12th Earl of Derby.

Left: Camel-racing in the Egyptian city of Cairo was just one of the unusual contests which have involved birds and animals.

Right: Ostrich racing in Cape Province, South Africa, was an event which drew large crowds. Although ostriches have only two legs they can run very fast, being capable of speeds of 60 kilometres an hour.

Below: Sled-racing across the packed snow was a sport much favoured in 19th-century Russia. Teams of horses drew the sleds and their drivers at great speeds. This sport was later transferred to Canada and Alaska, but here the sleds were drawn by teams of dogs. 'Dog derbies' were held, covering hundreds of kilometres.

Driven Horse-Racing

Driven horse-racing with lightweight but specially reinforced vehicles is an exciting but dangerous sport. There is a great risk of injury for the drivers as they struggle for a good position on the rails. The vehicles may collide or become locked together.

Horses in driven-horse races have to be both fast and strong. Their riders must keep a cool head at all times and have a very good sense of judgement. They must sense when there

is an opening into which they can take both horse and vehicle at speed.

One of the driven horses in this race has become entangled in the reins. The driver will have to use all his skill and his experience in order to regain control of his vehicle.

Good drivers have always commanded high salaries to ride for their owners. At the beginning of the 20th century an American, Will Caton, was driving in races for the Czar of Russia. He won more than 2,000 races for his royal master and was paid £10,000 a year and 15 per cent of the prize money. After the Russian Revolution in 1917 he was imprisoned, but managed to escape.

27

Winter Sports
Skating

Winter sports is the name generally given to those sports held on snow and ice. They are usually associated with the colder parts of the Northern Hemisphere. In the Winter Games of the Olympics, held every four years since 1924, the speed sports commonly included are skating, skiing and bob-sledding.

Speed-skating is thought to have originated on the frozen canals of Holland in the Middle Ages, and to have been introduced to England by European workers brought in to build canals in East Anglia. The first iron skates were devised in 1572, and a skating club was established in Scotland seventy years later. The Scots took the sport to North America.

Right: Two contestants compete in the world speed-skating championships in Paris in 1981. The championships have been held since 1893. Top-class male and female skaters train for up to five hours a day.

Below: This is a 16th-century skating scene. The first skaters in Holland and Scandinavia used skates made from the bones of animals. These were followed by wooden-bladed skates. It was in Scotland that skating really became a sport.

Speed-skating events in the world championships are held over 500, 1,500, 5,000 and 10,000 metres for men; and 500, 1,000, 1,500, 3,000 and 5,000 metres for women. Speed-skating tracks are usually oblong in shape and cover 400 metres. Races are held in heats, with two competitors in each heat. Racing skates have long, thin blades of aluminium attached to strong, lightweight boots. A speed skater needs enormous power in the legs to be able to thrust off with each foot.

The sport received a boost which made it more popular in 1850, when E.W. Bushnell of Philadelphia invented a pair of skates with steel blades. These did not have to be sharpened almost every time they were used, as had been the case with the iron variety.

One of the greatest of all skaters was the Canadian, Norval Baptie. After winning amateur championships, he turned professional and toured the United States of America. Unfortunately he was much too fast for the other professional skaters, so Baptie had to become a figure skater instead. He gave exhibitions of this art and made a living in this way.

29

Sail-Skating

Sail-skating is the sport of sailing on ice skates. In the right weather conditions, the sails catch the wind and the vehicle speeds across snow and ice. Old prints show a form of the sport being carried out on frozen lake surfaces in Europe in the Middle Ages. By the end of the 19th century the sport was a popular one in the USA, as this illustration of the Hudson river shows.

Skiing

Skiing has been used as a form of transport in snowbound countries for thousands of years. It can be traced back to prehistoric times, when people moved across the frozen countryside on skis made from the large bones of animals. Thousands of years later, in the 13th century AD, King Swerre of Sweden found himself marooned with his troops in deep snow at the Battle of Oslo. He managed to keep in touch with the enemy's movements by sending out scouts on reconnoitres. The scouts were mounted on skis.

As a sport, however, skiing has been in existence for little more than a century. It owed its early development to a Norwegian called Sondre Nordheim. In the 1840s, he introduced flexible thongs to bind the skis more securely to the feet of skiers. This enabled them to go more quickly and to jump greater distances. This led to the establishment of ski races, the first of which seems to have been held in Norway in 1866. In the next year the first ski club in the USA was formed.

Today there are a number of different events in which skiers may take part, and their skis, varying in length, can be made of wood, metal or plastic. In addition to their skis, skiers also carry a wooden or metal stick in each hand. These sticks are used to provide balance, support, thrust, grip and direction.

Downhill racing occurs over snow-covered slopes which are usually between 500 and 800 metres long and covered with obstacles in the form of snow mounds. *Cross-country racing* is held over much longer courses, consisting of both slopes and level ground. The *slalom* is a time-trial over a course containing a drop of about 150 metres. Competitors have to wind in and out of pairs of flag-poles in a race against the clock.

Cross-country skiing, also known as Nordic skiing, has become very popular in recent years. Competitive cross-country skiing events draw large crowds along the route – so many skiers together make a beautiful sight.

Short-distance events down slopes are known as Alpine events. The longer, or 'Nordic' races across country vary in distance from 5 to 50 kilometres. A great advance in Alpine skiing took place in Switzerland in 1921. A prominent British skier, Arnold Lunn, decided that the downhill events did not test the control of the skiers sufficiently. Accordingly he devised the *slalom*, in which skiers had to make their way at great speed between flags which were placed at intervals on the slope.

Below: The 'flying kilometre' is another name given to the downhill race. Competitors are allowed to gather speed and are then timed down a very steep slope. Skis worn for this event are heavy, and the racers crouch to present as little resistance as possible to the wind. Great speeds can be reached in this way.

Right: Speed skiing requires a great deal of equipment, some of it expensive. Different types of ski are needed, according to the event being entered. They range in length from 180 to 210 centimetres. The ends are turned up to prevent the skis digging into the snow. The soles are often waxed. Skiers also need special suits and helmets.

One of the most unusual of skiing events is the one known as the *biathlon*. This is held over a course of 20 kilometres across country. It is based on a Scandinavian military exercise. Skiers in this event carry rifles and ammunition. After 4 kilometres they have to lie down and fire five shots at a target. After 8 kilometres they fire at another target from a standing position. Again at 12 kilometres they lie down and fire five shots at a target. At 16 kilometres they fire while standing up. Points are deducted for every shot which misses its target. The object of the competition is to be the first to arrive at the winning-post and to score as high as possible with each shot.

Although basic skiing techniques have changed little over the years, technological advances have done a lot for the sport. This is particularly true of the development of cable-cars and other mechanical means which transport skiers quickly to the tops of slopes, thus increasing the number of runs they can make down.

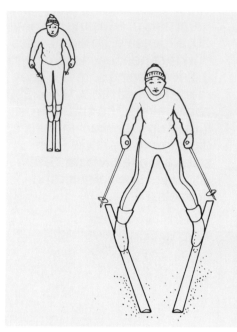

When the first European settlers reached Canada in the 16th century, they found that the Indians were competing in snowshoe races over long distances as one of their major sports. These shoes were very broad across the base so that the wearers did not sink into the snow-drifts. The French who settled in Quebec took up the sport, and, presently, many clubs devoted to this strange form of skiing were formed in Canada.

Some skiing champions have become enormously popular with people all over the world. Two of them, Toni Sailer and Jean-Claude Killy, introduced new styles of skiing which pleased the crowds and made them exciting to see in action. Sailer, an Austrian, won a number of world titles, and in the 1956 Winter Olympics gained gold medals in the slalom, giant slalom and downhill events. Jean-Claude Killy, a Frenchman, won three Olympic gold medals at the 1968 Winter Games, and has also gained several world titles over the years.

Left: This snowshoe steeplechase, held in 19th-century Canada, was typical of the events engaged in by the French who settled in that country. Snowshoe races became particularly popular among women. It was one of the first outdoor sporting events in which they took part in the New World. Such races became popular social events and drew large crowds.

Right: There are two slalom events, the slalom and the giant slalom. In the former, a competitor has to negotiate two different courses, each of about 575 metres, with a drop of between 150 and 200 metres. About 75 'gates' or pairs of flags have to be negotiated. The giant slalom is longer, about 1,500 metres, with about 60 to 70 gates.

Between 1934 and 1939, a woman skier from Germany, Christel Cranz, won four slalom world titles, three downhill titles and five in the combined events. She also won a gold medal at the 1936 Olympics.

36

Left: It is very important for a skier to be able to stop at will. A common method is for the skier to force out his heels and bring the tips of his skis together in a 'snowplough'. The movement is called this because it creates the same effect as a snowplough in the snow.

Above: The basic skiing movement along the flat is made up of a gliding movement, with the weight being transferred from one leg to the other in an economical, labour-saving action. This movement can be maintained over long distances with ease.

Machines on Ice

Some of the speed sports carried out on snow and ice have been really unusual. In 1970, a Japanese skier, Yuchiro Huira, skied down a large section of Mount Everest. Two years later a man called Rick Sylvester skied off the edge of a cliff in California more than 1,000 metres high. He was wearing a parachute, which opened at about 500 metres from the ground.

Machines, too, have been used to attain great speeds over snow and ice. Sleds and toboggans have been used for many years, but one of the latest vehicles is the ski-bob. This is something like a bicycle with the wheels replaced by skis. A ski-bob run is no more than five kilometres long and has a drop of about 400 metres.

Another spectacular form of transport over snow and ice is skijoring. This is like water-skiing, only it takes place on land. A skier is pulled at speed by a horse, a car or even, in some cases, by a low-flying aircraft.

Right: This is the start of a bobsleigh race at St Moritz. The steel bobsleigh is propelled at an incredible speed down the run by two-and four-man crews. The riders push the sleigh at the start, while holding on to handles at the side and rear, and then leap into it as it gathers speed. The course is at least 1,500 metres long and banked.

Below: The Japanese team in the luge event in the 1976 Olympics. The luge is a toboggan or sled with no form of mechanical steering or brake. It is operated by the feet and a hand rope. There are events for single-seater and two-man luges. Riders sit down, leaning backwards.

The sport of tobogganing is believed to have originated in Switzerland in the 1850s, when snowbound tourists constructed a few sleds and used them to coast down the gentler surrounding slopes. The sport caught on, and in 1881, the first championships were held at Davos.

Toboggans had been used as a means of transport in northern Europe for thousands of years, so the sport was quick to spread to Austria, Germany and Scandinavia. As usual science came to the assistance of sport, and in the 1930s an Austrian invented a more flexible sled which could be controlled by the driver, instead of by mechanical means, as had previously been the case.

Over the years the sport settled down into three main sections. The *bobsleigh*, in which participants are not allowed to use brakes except in an emergency, has to be steered with the greatest accuracy. If it touches the side banking, precious moments may be lost. The *luge toboggan* has front runners which are moved by delicate pressure from the driver. The *Cresta toboggan* consists of a platform mounted on two steel runners. The rider lies flat on the platform on his stomach.

Left: A two-man luge toboggan in action on a Swedish run. A speed of almost 130 kilometres an hour has been attained by experts on a luge. A luge run is steeper than a bobsleigh run and has narrower corners to negotiate. Each toboggan in a competition makes four runs, and the aggregate times are worked out to decide the winners.

Below: A snowmobile hurtles across the snow and ice in Canada. It is controlled by handlebars linked to the skis. The driver has to keep shifting position in order to get the maximum speed out of the vehicle. There are brake controls on the handlebars together with throttle.

Sooner or later, speed sports enthusiasts always manage to think up ways of racing vehicles against each other – even the most unlikely ones. This was certainly the case with the snowmobile. The first of these machines was built in the 1920s. It consisted of a sled with an engine attached, and the whole contraption was steered by a ski. By 1960, the development of small, high-powered engines led to the construction of powerful one- and two-man snowmobiles. These could be driven across the snow at high speeds.

Almost at once snowmobile races were being held in Northern Europe and North America. The more powerful entrants were capable of being driven at speeds of up to 160 kilometres an hour. In the hands of inefficient or inexperienced competitors they were extremely dangerous. This led to a demand for the sport to be more closely supervised and controlled, after there had been a number of accidents at high speed on ice and snow.

Children on Ice and Snow

Winter sports require great skill if they are to be performed properly. Most of the best skiers and skaters begin to practice at a very early age. This of course gives an advantage to children who live in the colder areas of the world. Surrounded by snow and ice, they have the chance to use skis and skates while they are still very young. If they show promise they are noticed and given the opportunity to be coached to a high standard. This is particularly true of Russia. There, there are many special schools and athletes are sent to them at an early age for specialist training if they show enough promise.

Below: Children ride across the snow in Austria. A story dating back to the 15th century tells of a 16-year-old girl, Liedwi, who fell and broke a rib while skating. She spent the rest of her life in a convent. After her death she was made the patron saint of skaters. There are many such stories about young people and winter sports in the mountainous countries of Europe. Most champion skiers and skaters come from these snowy areas.

Right: This young speed-skater is warmly wrapped up, but in a streamlined fashion, so that he can cut through the air as quickly as possible. There are many skills that he will have to learn. He must develop the muscles of his legs in order to have the strength to thrust off vigorously with either foot. Each foot must pass the other with the least possible amount of space between them. He must learn to balance his body over his skating leg as he moves. He will have to practise moving smoothly and with great economy.

Wheels
Cycling

In 1690 in Paris, an inventor called Monsieur de Sivrac displayed a machine consisting of two wooden wheels joined by a crossbar. The 'rider' saddled the crossbar and then moved the machine by pushing with his feet. It was not until 1818 that another Frenchman, the Baron de Saverbrum, invented the forerunner of the penny-farthing bicycle, with a large front wheel and a small rear one.

The first race on record took place in France in 1868, and was won by an Englishman, James Moore. In 1884, an American, Thomas Stevens, set out to ride a penny-farthing cycle with solid rubber tyres round the world. He returned several years later to claim that he had cycled 'everywhere there was land'. Modern cycling was heralded in 1885 by the invention in England of a bicycle with two wheels that were almost the same size. This made speed-cycling possible and encouraged bicycle racing.

Right: The Tour de France in June 1981. This is perhaps the most famous of all long-distance professional cycling races. The route usually covers more than 4,000 kilometres and the race lasts for almost a month. It is divided into stages. The winner of each stage is allowed to wear a yellow jersey the following day. Racers ride in teams which are sponsored by big companies.

Below: Eddy Merckx, a rider from Belgium, won more than 300 professional races, including four consecutive first places in the Tour de France.

Above: A cycling race is in progress. Road races take place over many different distances, from 32 kilometres up to thousands of kilometres. Track events range from short sprints to 100-kilometre competitions.

Left: Reg Harris was an outstanding British sprinter. He won cycling world titles as an amateur and as a professional, and took two silver medals at the 1948 Olympics.

Below: Tandem racing was just one of the cycling events included in the Olympic Games. Tandems are elongated versions of ordinary racing cycles, with a frame reinforced to carry two riders. In a tandem team, each person has special duties. The front rider is in charge, deciding when to spurt. The rider behind is there to provide the extra power and also to keep a look-out for sprints by other racers, so that the front rider can be warned in time. Tandem racing is a good example of teamwork.

Cycling tracks are oval in shape but also have two areas which are straight, one at the finishing-line and the other in the back straight. The track is banked.

In the 1890s indoor cycle races became popular in the USA. Some of them involved penny-farthings, while others featured the new smaller-wheeled bicycles which could go much faster.

The most eagerly followed events were the six-day races held for professionals at Madison Square Gardens in New York. A cyclist had to ride for a total of 142 hours, not counting rest periods. The winner was the one covering the most ground. In 1893, Albert Shock won a major event on a small-wheeled bicycle. Almost at once the penny-farthings went out of fashion.

While the professionals continued to race indoors, road racing became the favourite sport of amateur cyclists. In the 1920s and 1930s cycling as a speed sport lost favour, the emphasis being on road touring, whole families taking part. Today both track racing and road racing are extremely popular around the world.

The sprint events in cycling are held over 1,000 metres for single events, and 2,000 metres for those involving tandems. There are also *time-trials*, in which individual competitors ride against the clock. Other track events for both amateurs and professionals are the *pursuit* ones. In a pursuit race the riders start on opposite sides of the track. When the race begins they set off at a great pace, chasing each other. A successful pursuit rider will overhaul his opponent or at least get very close to him.

Over longer distances there are *motor-paced* events. Each cyclist is paced by a small motorcycle just ahead of him throughout the race. An elimination track cycle race is the one known as the *devil-take-the-hindmost*. A number of cyclists set off together. Every so often, after an agreed number of laps, the last man to cross the line is eliminated until there are just two riders left to fight it out.

In road races a great deal depends upon tactics. Most of these races are held over long distances, so the riders have to decide when to sprint and when to keep in with the pack. In road races in which teams take part, each team usually tries to decide in advance which of their riders will be supported by the rest. It is then the task of the supporting riders to protect the 'star' of the team, pacing him and trying to see to it that he gets every advantage.

Left: All sorts of hazards are met with in cyclo-cross races. They are held in the winter months over ground frequently churned up by storms. Only a third of any course is laid over roads. The rest is held over hills, valleys, rivers and similar obstacles. Riders do their best to get off to a fast start and then maintain their lead.

Above: The British National Cyclo-Cross Championships held in 1977. The most successful contestants are those who can keep riding for the longest periods of time and who do not have to waste time in mounting and dismounting their cycles. In major contests, riders are allowed to use fresh cycles if they damage theirs.

Cyclo-cross is a sport held over extremely rough ground in the winter months. Cyclists have to cover a cross-country course littered with obstacles, both natural and man-made. They ride whenever they can, but when the going gets too rough they dismount and carry their cycles on their shoulders. Races usually consist of a number of laps around a course of no more than 24 kilometres. Each cyclo-cross race has a massed start, usually in a field.

Motorcycle Racing

Although motor-cars were developed before motorcycles, it is sometimes claimed that the motorcycle came first. Gottlieb Daimler perfected the internal combustion engine for cars in Germany in 1885. But as an experiment he fixed it to his bicycle, thus inventing the motorcycle!

By the beginning of the 20th century, motorcycles were competing with cars in fast, furious and highly dangerous races, organized on public roads in North America and Europe. The first major organized races for motorcycles alone were held in France. The construction of special circuits in many countries helped the sport to grow.

Manufacturing companies all over the world developed their own motorcycles, and then entered them in races, hoping to benefit from the publicity. Reliability trials were held over public roads. These were in reality races, with the riders employed by the factories doing everything they could to win for their owners.

Motor-cross is a form of motorcycle racing which takes place over rough cross-country courses. There are events for motor-cycles with sidecars (left) and for single machines (below). An agreed number of laps have to be completed. A good start is essential because parts of the course are very narrow and riders almost have to queue up to enter these bottle-necks. Machines which are entered for these races have to be very strong, with highly-tuned engines and very fit drivers. The first motor-cross events were held in Yorkshire when employees of a motor-cycle manufacturer raced their machines over rough ground. Today events are held all over the world.

Speedway racing takes place between teams of motor-cyclists on cinders, or 'dirt-tracks', over courses of varying shapes. After football it is the most popular sport among spectators in Britain. Speedway had its origins in a crude way in the USA in 1910, but achieved real fame a few years later in Australia.

In Britain, the first experimental meetings took place in 1927. A year later a speedway meeting at London's White City attracted a crowd of 78,000 people. After the Second World War there were more than 35 stadiums in Great Britain holding regular speedway meetings, and drawing millions of spectators each year.

In a typical league competition between two teams there will be four riders in each race, two from each side. They will line up behind a set of tapes, taking it in turn to get the inside lane position. When the tapes are raised the race begins. The race take place in an anti-clockwise direction and each rider does his best to get to the first bend in front of the others. In most team matches there are 13 races, each one consisting of four laps.

Above: In some Scandinavian countries, speedway races are held on ice, making the motorcycles even more difficult to control. Speedway racing is very popular on the Continent, and top-class riders can earn as much as £1,000 for a single night's work. However, their expenses are high. A good quality leather riding-suit may cost more than £100, and a suitable helmet more than half that much.

Right: In addition to speedway riding, road-racing is also popular with spectators. Some races are held over public roads which have been cleared for the occasion, while others take place over special circuits with specially designed twists and bends.

Road-racing, or circuit-racing, developed steadily during the 20th century. Events were held for motorcycles with different-sized engines. In 1907, the first Tourist Trophy race was held over the roads of the Isle of Man, and was followed by other national races. The motorcycle manufacturers competed with one another to see which could win the most events in the different engine categories. In the 1920s, British riders on Nortons did well, while in the 1930s the German and Italian machines won many races. By the 1960s, Japanese motorcycles were supreme in the world.

Other motorcycle sports include *trials*, in which the entrants compete over sections of a course, before judges, in an effort to make as few handling mistakes as possible. Sprint races are held over grass courses. Endurance events take place over long distances, usually on roads. In sidecar-racing, highly-specialized 'racing chairs' are attached to the motorcycles.

Motor-Racing

The first petrol-driven cars were developed in the 1880s. Before the end of the century, races were being held on roads between different towns in North America and Europe. At first, vehicles driven by steam and electricity were triumphant, but by 1900 petrol-driven cars were supreme. Races on public roads were discontinued when they became too dangerous for the spectators crowding on the verges.

More remote venues were sought. In the USA, the sand beaches of Daytona in Florida, and the salt flats of the town of Bonneville in Utah were favoured. Cars were tested and raced over the measured mile (1.609 kilometres). All too often a race was lost because a car broke down or developed a flat tyre. Designers and mechanics demanded facilities to repair and service vehicles during the actual races. This led to the construction of enclosed race circuits, with 'pits' for the mechanics, where drivers pulled in during a race.

Right: A driver makes a pit-stop during a race. The teams of mechanics servicing each car can work at incredible speed, changing wheels and making minor repairs.

Below left: The start of a race at Brooklands, outside London, in 1923. This was the world's first specially constructed racing track, opened in 1907. Speeds of 240 kph were reached. The track remained open for years, but had to close in the end when people living nearby complained about the noise!

Below right: An exciting moment in the Dutch Grand Prix of 1981. The course lap distance is 4.14 kilometres.

Most countries now stage major motor-racing events. Top-line drivers travel the world to take part in them, and try to gain enough points to win the World Championship. These races are usually known as Grand Prix events; they are named after the Grand Prix de Pau, which was held in 1901.

International events are divided into categories which are based on the size and strength of the cars and their engines. The most important are known as Formula One races. Teams of cars are entered by manufacturers or wealthy private owners. The cars are painted in various colours, a different one for each nation. The British colour is green, the American blue and white, the French blue, and so on.

Great safety precautions are taken at Grand Prix events, because so many cars hurtling round circuits of five or six kilometres, for distances of up to 650 kilometres, can get into trouble and crash. In 1955 in a 24-hour event at Le Mans in France, a Mercedes driven by Pierre Levegh crashed into the crowd, killing more than 80 spectators. This caused a great deal of controversy, and Switzerland banned motor-racing as a result, saying that it was much too dangerous for drivers and crowds.

Above: A six-hour race being held at Silverstone in 1981. This is the fastest racing track in Great Britain. A Grand Prix event is held here in alternate years. The circuit is 4.6 kilometres. Before being converted for racing it was used as an airfield.

Above: Jackie Ickx drives a
Porsche at Le Mans in 1981.
This course was once famous
for its sprint start, in which the
drivers had to run to their cars.

Below: A stock car, a normal
car strengthened for a race,
catches fire on the track.

Today most cars are raced on permanent tracks, but some
are held on ordinary roads which have been closed for the
occasion. On the tracks there are races for many kinds of cars
– sports models, stock cars, as well as for different types of
racing models.

There are also long distance rallies. These take place over
several stages, with control-points along the route. Perhaps
the most famous of these is the East African rally. It takes
place in Kenya and Uganda and lasts four days. Standard
cars, greatly reinforced, have to pass over poor roads,
deserts, rock-piles, and through jungles full of wild animals.
On rallies like this the driver is always accompanied by a
navigator who must plot the course, study the maps and give
directions.

There have been a number of long-distance rallies over
the last few decades. In 1970, there was a World Cup rally, to
mark the football tournament, from London to Mexico.
Probably the wildest of all long-distance events, however,
took place in 1907. The internal combustion engine was only
just over 20 years old, yet this race was held between Peking
in China and Paris in France. The winner completed the
course in two months!

Drag-car racing originated in the USA, but has recently started to find favour among spectators in Europe. A drag car, or 'hot rod', is very long, with large soft rear tyres and small front ones. Races are held over very short distances between two drag cars at a time. These machines have tremendous acceleration and leap off at the start. The courses are only about 400 metres long, and so powerful are the hot-rods that they can cover the course in as little as six seconds.

Go-kart racing began in the USA between the wars, when most drivers could not affort the massive racing-cars used in Grand Prix and similar events. Instead they built tiny open carts powered by lawn-mower engines. At first, races were held on remote roads and in public parks. They became popular and began to race on proper tracks. Soon special engines were designed for them and championships were inaugurated.

Right: An entrant in the East African rally. Such cars have had many modifications. They are built for strength and also for endurance. Inside the car there is an instrument known as a 'Halda'. Not only does this show the distance covered but it also converts it, so that the driver and navigator can see what their average speed is.

Below: Many well-known major racing drivers got their start in go-kart racing. As these vehicles do not have clutches, they cannot start quickly. Drivers are allowed one lap in which to gather speed and then enter the race with a 'flying start'. Speeds of more than 100 kilometres an hour may be reached in go-karts.

Above: *Thunderbird* was a well-known hot-rod of the 1970s. Although drag races are over in seconds, they are exciting to watch because of the sheer power expended at the start. The front wheels rear in the air when the power is turned on and the race begins.

Because they are so slender, hot rods are sometimes called 'rails' by their drivers. There are different types of hot-rods. One category is simply known as 'funny cars'. Their owners compete to see who can build the most powerful dragster!

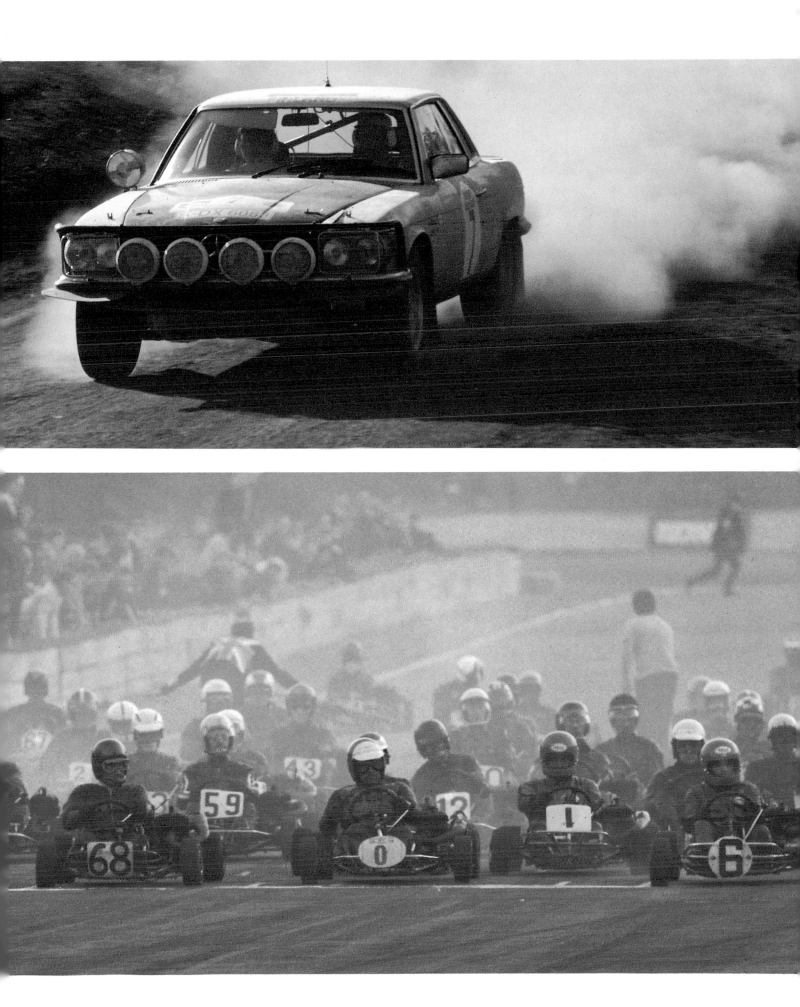

Left: Two cars in an autocross event race against each other and the clock. The field is marked out with flags and bales of straw. Each car races twice round a course of three to five laps. The one with the best time is the winner.

Below left: In sidecar-racing a great deal depends upon the agility of the rider in the sidecar, who has to transfer his weight from side to side at crucial moments.

Below right: European speed roller-skating champion Mike McGough seen at full stretch. World championships are held for men at 1,000, 5,000, 10,000 and 20,000 metres, and for women at 500, 3,000 and 5,000 metres. The rules of the sport follow those of ice-skating.

People have turned the most surprising and unusual events into speed sports. In the 1860s, for example, in Belgium and Holland, ice-skaters wishing to practise on land experimented with skates on wheels. Twenty years later, an American invented the smooth-running ball-bearing roller skate. By 1894, the first British one-mile speed roller-skating championships were being held and another speed sport was under way.

In Canada, one of the tasks of a lumberjack was to propel enormous felled tree trunks down rivers to the rail heads. Men would sometimes race one another *en route*. Eventually these impromptu events became part of the very popular World Lumberjack Championships.

At these big events the most popular speed sport is still the *long-poling* race. Competitors each stand on a log with a long pole in their hands. When the race starts they dig their poles into the water and set off down the river of great speed towards the winning-post, while trying to keep their balance on the slippery logs.

Land Records

The development of the motor-car industry owed much to the efforts of the brave drivers who raced the pioneer models and attempted to set new land speed records. The first great automobile manufacturers wanted both to test their engines under conditions of great stress and to gain the maximum amount of publicity for their cars. The best way to achieve this was to attempt to set new world records.

At first there was competition between cars with steam-engines, those powered by petrol and ones propelled by electricity. The first vehicle to exceed 100 kilometres an hour was driven by electricity. By the beginning of the 20th century, however, petrol-powered cars were the ones breaking the old records and setting new ones.

The first really fast cars were European in origin, but then automobile racing and record attempts became very popular in the United States. American manufacturers set out to design cars which would take the records away from the Europeans. At first all records were set over the distance of one mile, as it was considered highly dangerous to drive a car at high speeds any farther than this. Then the distance was changed to a 'flying kilometre', the car being allowed to gather speed and thus getting a flying start.

Today, land speed records are supervised by the international organization known as the *Fédération Internationale de l'Automobile*. A car is allowed two attempts with a flying start, either over one mile or one kilometre in opposite directions, the average time of the two runs being worked out for the record.

Memorable records

Year	Vehicle	Driver	Speed (kph)
1898	*Jeantaud*	Comte de Chasseloup-Laubat	63.16
1902	*Mors*	H. Fournier	123.27
1906	*Stanley*	F. Marriott	195.65
1911	*Benz*	S. Burman	227.51
1925	*Sunbeam*	M. Campbell	242.63
1929	*Golden Arrow*	H. Segrave	372.47
1935	*Bluebird*	M. Campbell	484.62
1939	*Railton*	J. Cobb	594.99
1964	*Bluebird*	D. Campbell	648.73
1965	*Spirit of America*	C. Breedlove	966.57
1970	*Blue Flame*	C. Gabelich	1,001.78

Above: Sheets of metal being placed beneath the wheels of Sir Malcolm Campbell's *Sunbeam* to prevent it sinking into the sand, during his successful attempt on the land speed record in 1925.

Left: The *Blue Flame* setting a new land speed record in 1970 at Bonneville Salt Flats, Utah, one of the few areas with enough space.

Below: Stan Barrett's powerful rocket-car has four wheels, so it qualifies as a 'car'.

Racing in the Air

Ballooning

In 1782, two Frenchmen, the Montgolfier brothers, began experimenting with hot air as a means of propelling objects into the air. They reasoned that as hot air was lighter than the cold air surrounding it, hot air contained in an envelope of some sort would rise. At first they confined their experiments to holding open paper-bags over coal-fires until they filled with hot air and ascended.

In 1783 they constructed a huge balloon made of paper between layers of linen. They built a bonfire under the balloon, which expanded and rose into the air. Next the Montgolfiers sent a goat and some farmyard birds up in a basket attached to their hot-air balloon, and followed this by sending people aloft. The original bonfire method of filling the balloon with hot air was replaced by using the newly discovered gas, hydrogen, to fill it. The era of ballooning had begun.

It was not long before it was taken up as a sport. An American newspaper publisher living in Paris, James Gordon Bennett, donated a trophy for ballooning, for which different nations could compete. Long-distance races became popular. As balloonists had little control over the direction they took, the prizes were usually given for the balloon which was able to travel the farthest from the starting-point.

The sport received a setback in 1933, when at the start of an international competition in Belgium an electrical storm struck the balloons as they rose into the air, ripping ten of them to shreds. Five of the pilots were killed. Some hot-air balloon have been kept aloft for more than eight hours. The really skilful balloonist is the man or woman who can keep the balloon travelling in a straight line.

Right: There are different types of balloon-racing. One of them involves each pilot declaring where he or she intends to land. Points are then given to the one who gets closest to the declared landing-point. A balloon may cost about £2,000.

Aviation Racing

After 1903, when the Wright brothers flew the first heavier-than-air machine at Kittyhawk in the USA, many fliers attempted to set speed records and to fly faster than competitors from point to point. In an attempt to further the development of aviation, a number of prizes were offered for pilots who could complete certain routes.

In June 1927, an American, Charles Lindbergh, aroused a great deal of interest in aviation when he flew non-stop from New York to Paris on his own in 33 hours 29 minutes. The greatest of international air-racing events took place in 1934. To celebrate the centenary of the Australian state of Victoria, a race was arranged from Mildenhall in Suffolk to Melbourne in Australia. Twenty aircraft took part and the race was won by two Britons, C.W. Scott and T. Campbell Black, who completed the course in 71 hours and 18 seconds.

A friend of the Wrights, Octave Chanute, a Frenchman living in the USA wrote after their flight, 'The machines will eventually be fast, they will be used in sport.'

Above: Charles Lindbergh, the first pilot to fly solo across the Atlantic, arriving in his famous aircraft, *The Spirit of St Louis*.

Left: The *Gee Bee Super Sportster* flying in the 1935 Bendix race in the USA. The development of these small, relatively inexpensive aircraft in the 1930s led to many races being organized. The world's first major organized air-race took place in Rheims in 1909. In 1913, the Schneider Trophy event was inaugurated. This was intended for seaplanes. Entrants had to be tested for sea-worthiness, and there was a race round a course.

Right: Amy Johnson was the most famous of British women fliers. With great determination she took flying lessons while working at an ordinary job, and later made famous solo flights to South Africa, India and Australia. In 1932 she married another well-known aviator, Jim Mollison. They flew the Atlantic together but were injured in a crash-landing.

Below: In 1919 the *Daily Mail* offered a prize of £10,000 for the first successful flight across the Atlantic. It was won by Captain Alcock and Lieutenant Brown, flying a bi-plane. They left Newfoundland and 16 hours later crash-landed in Galway, Ireland. The two men were knighted for their achievement.

GREAT AIR RACES

For the first 40 years of powered flight, pilots competed in many speed events, sometimes against other aircraft, sometimes in races against the clock.

1909 Louis Blériot of France wins the £10,000 *Daily Mail* prize for the first flight across the English Channel – 50 kilometres in 40 minutes.

1919 Alcock and Brown of Great Britain win the £10,000 *Daily Mail* prize for the first non-stop crossing of the Atlantic – 3150 kilometres in 16 hours 28 minutes.

1927 Charles Lindbergh of the USA wins the $25,000 Orteig Prize for the first direct, non-stop flight from New York to Paris – 33 hours 39 minutes.

1927 Charles Kingsford Smith of Australia and his crew make the first successful crossing of the Pacific, from California to Australia in three 'hops', a total of 12,315 kilometres in an airborne time of 83 hours 42 minutes.

1932 Jim Mollison of Great Britain makes the first solo non-stop crossing of the Atlantic from east to west, flying 3,300 kilometres from Ireland to New Brunswick in 30 hours 15 minutes.

1934 C.W. Scott and Thomas Black of Great Britain win the £10,000 Robertson Prize for winning the race from England to Australia – 18,000 kilometres in 2 days 22 hours 59 minutes.

1936 C.W. Scott and Giles Guthrie of Great Britain win the England-South Africa air-race in 2 days 4 hours 57 minutes.

On 17 December 1907 Wilbur and Orville Wright made four flights in a heavier-than-air machine. These took place near Kitty Hawk, North Carolina and were the world's first powered and controlled flights. The longest of these first flights lasted for 59 seconds.

Gliding

A number of aviation pioneers experimented with aircrafts without engines – gliders. Perhaps the best-known was the German, Otto Lilienthal. He made his first flight in 1890. He was attached to a contraption consisting of a harness and wings. He ran down the side of a hill as fast as he could, and jumped into the air, moving his dangling legs in order to steer this primitive glider. He later died of injuries which he sustained in a crash.

Below: Gliding became very popular in Germany after the First World War. The Germans were not allowed to build aircraft with engines, in case they used them for warlike purposes. Instead they concentrated on gliders, like this Fokker, which is being flown by the inventor at a competition.

Left: Most modern gliders are made of fibre-glass and epoxy resin. They are launched from a winch, or by being towed by a car. Sometimes an aircraft is used to tow the glider, in order to gain great heights. Competitions are not so much for speed, although this helps, but to see how much altitude may be gained and how far the glider can soar. After the pilot has been released from the towline, he or she must turn in the air to find favourable air currents. Champion pilots have achieved altitudes of more than 14,000 metres.

In the Water
Swimming

Thrashing through swimming-pools for short distances, or surging across rivers, lakes and even seas, men and women have tested their strength and skill in the water for thousands of years. There are four basic swimming strokes.

The fastest is the *front crawl*, combining an overarm stroke with the fluttering up and down of the extended legs. In the *butterfly stroke* a racer lifts both hands and arms out of the water and then drives them back towards the waist. The *backstroke* consists of the swimmer lying on his back and using a flutter kick up and down, while alternately stretching each arm straight back, before pulling it back in line with the hips. In the *breast stroke* the swimmer extends both arms and sweeps them out and back, drawing both legs up and pushing them out.

Below: Captain Matthew Webb, the first man to swim the English Channel, is seen here stopping to drink some hot coffee during his attempt. It was his second try and he set out on 24 August 1875 from Dover. He used both the breast and side strokes in his attempt, and smeared himself in advance with porpoise oil. A lugger and two small boats accompanied him on his swim. The captain did not pay much attention to the currents and tides in his planning. As a result he was swept kilometres out of his way. However he succeeded in his task.

Men and women took to the water quite early in history. Cave drawings scratched on to rocks in North Africa more than 11,000 years ago depict swimmers. An Egyptian aristocrat writing more than 2,000 years before the birth of Christ described his children's swimming lessons. Swimming became part of the training of Assyrian warriors, so that they could pursue their foes across rivers. For thousands of years swimming was both a popular hobby and a keenly contested competitive sport.

In the 1870s, an English swimming enthusiast, Frederick Cavill, visited the Solomon Islands in the South Pacific. He noticed that the islanders were using a stroke he had not seen before. When Cavill opened a swimming school in Australia, he introduced the new stroke. It became known as the 'Australian crawl' and was used to break world records at the turn of the century.

Above: One of the world's most famous swimmers was the great American, Johnny Weissmuller. In the 1924 and 1928 Olympics he won a total of five gold medals and broke 24 world records. When he retired from swimming he went to Hollywood and became a film star, playing the part of Tarzan, king of the jungle. He became famous for his jungle yell, his method of swinging from tree to tree – and his impressive swimming style.

The home of organized modern swimming is generally held to be Australia. National championships were being competed for there in the 1840s. British championships were swum in the River Thames in 1877, and the first American national events were celebrated a few years later in New York. But it was Australia which produced many of the first great champions and coaches.

After the English emigrant Frederick Cavill had taken the crawl stroke from the South Seas to Australia, his six sons began winning events with it all over the world. One of them, Richard, won the British 100 yards (91.4 metres) freestyle event with it in 1902, in a time of 58.6 seconds. In the following year Richard's brother Sydney was appointed coach of the famous Olympic Club in San Francisco. He was there for 25 years and trained generations of young American swimmers, including many champions.

In 1913, however, the world record was broken by a swimmer who had not been trained by Cavill. This was a young man from Hawaii, Duke Kahanamoku, who held the world title for five years. It was noticed that the islander used the crawl style. When asked who had taught it to him, he replied that no one had given him lessons in it; the method had been used in his home islands for hundreds of years. The Hawaiian remained the word's best sprint swimmer until an American, Johnny Weissmuller took over. Weissmuller later became famous for his role as Tarzan in many films.

Left: Shane Gould of Australia won three gold medals, a silver and a bronze at the 1972 Olympic Games, before she was 16 years old. Altogether in her brief amateur career she broke 11 world records. Her opponents were so apprehensive of her, that at the Munich Olympics some of them wore T-shirts with the inscription 'All that glitters is not Gould!' Shane was expected to do even better at the 1976 Olympics, but at 16 she turned professional.

Long distance competitive swimming takes place over a number of different types of open water, including seas and inlets. There are also races across lakes and down rivers. Sometimes swimmers compete against each other, at other times they are racing against the clock, or just trying to complete a course.

Since Captain Webb swam the English Channel in 1875, hundreds of others have completed the course. The first woman swimmer to accomplish the crossing was the American Gertrude Ederle in 1926. One of the greatest long-distance swimmers was the Indian, Mihir Sen, who swam from Sri Lanka to India in 25 hours.

They are diving to start in the European championships of 1977. For international competitions, pools are usually 50 metres long and at least 21 metres wide. In all events a great deal depends upon getting a good start. Competitors try to enter the water with their bodies as flat as possible and with the maximum power to carry them forward. Swimmers are allowed to have two false starts to a race. At a third false start they are disqualified.

Swimmers and their coaches are always looking for ways of going faster through the water. This has sometimes led to disputes and controversy. As early as 1912, in the Olympic Games, an American swimmer called H.J. Hebner developed a backstroke style in which he used each arm alternately, instead of bringing them both over his head together, which was the usual method. Hebner won his final convincingly. His opponents protested, but the judges agreed that Hebner had broken no rules by employing his revolutionary style.

In 1956, a Japanese swimmer won an Olympic gold medal by swimming most of his breaststroke final under water. This method was then banned.

Sharron Davies (above) in the final of the Olympic backstroke in 1980. She was one of many fine women swimmers to win an Olympic gold medal. Before Sharron Davies, perhaps the most famous of all women swimmers was the Australian Dawn Fraser. She won the Olympic 100-metres title at three consecutive Olympic tournaments, in 1956, 1960 and 1964, breaking the world record for the distance nine times.

Above: Duncan Goodhew of the United Kingdom, swims in the 1977 European championships. Goodhew was one of the few British swimmers to do well in the 1980 Moscow Olympic Games, winning a gold medal in the breaststroke.

Right: Mark Spitz of the USA, seen here in the butterfly event. He won an unprecedented seven gold medals at the 1972 Olympics, to add to the two he had won earlier at the 1968 Mexico Olympics. After 1972, he turned professional.

Boats
Rowing and Sculling

The first boats propelled by oars were probably the barges powered by slaves in the Egyptian and Roman empires. The Romans brought the idea to England and, long before the Middle Ages, the rivers of Great Britain were full of small boats with rowers which could be hired to ferry passengers across. The River Thames in particular had many such oarsmen. In order to improve standards of safety, King Henry VIII ordered that only licensed men could ply for hire.

Some of these watermen began to race against one another for side-bets. In 1715, an actor called Thomas Doggett left a sum of money in his will for an annual race to be held from London Bridge to Chelsea between rowing-boats, each with a crew of six men.

College students took up this idea, and in 1829 there was the first meeting between crews from Oxford and Cambridge, the first university boat-race. Ten years later the first great regatta or rowing tournament was held at Henley on the River Thames.

Right: An event at the 1979 Henley regatta, the great international rowing and sculling tournament. It is held over the first four days in July and attracts entrants from all over the world.

Below left: A coracle race on the River Severn in 1881. These are small, round, wicker boats covered with animal skins. They were first used by fishermen on the rivers of Wales and Ireland, and they remain in use today. Races were once held on rivers and lakes.

Below right: A rowing event at the Soviet National Games of 1979.

Canoeing

Stone Age men and women were the first to use canoes, employing hollow logs or digging out tree-trunks to make them. They were used all over the world as a simple and effective method of water transport.

Canoes were first used for sport by a Scottish barrister, John Macgregor, who developed a type of canoe known as the Rob Roy and travelled all over Europe in it, later writing a book about his exploits. This led to the formation of the Royal Canoe Club, in London in 1865. The sport soon spread to the Continent and to the USA.

Canoeing became extremely popular in 1907, when a German called Hans Klepper opened a factory to manufacture a light folding canoe known as a kayak, based on the traditional Eskimo hunter's canoe.

Some canoes were used with sails, but paddle-operated ones were the most frequently used. In 1936, canoeing was introduced to the Olympic Games. Slalom events, paddling round carefully placed flags, and wild-water competitions were popular.

Above: A canoe race at the 1976 Olympics. Events are held for both single and double canoes. The use of fibre-glass canoes has improved speeds considerably.

Right: A competitor in the wild-water or white-water canoeing event. A canoeist has to paddle hard against the clock, passing natural obstacles in rough water.

Sailing

The first great international yachting competition took place in 1851 round the Isle of Wight, as part of the London Exposition of that year. All types of sailing vessels were allowed to take part over the 97-kilometre course in the English Channel, and the Royal Yacht Squadron donated a prize to the winner.

Sixteen years later the first trans-Atlantic race took place from the USA to Cowes on the Isle of Wight. Three vessels took part in dreadful weather conditions. The winner took 13 days to complete the course. The first yachting events at the Olympic Games took place in 1908, with events being held both in the Solent and the River Clyde. The development of small and relatively cheap sailing dinghies has made the sport the popular and widespread pastime that it has become today.

Above: Clare Francis, one of the greatest of single-handed round-the-world sailors, is seen before the start of a long-distance race.

Left: The annual Sydney to Hobart yacht race always starts on the morning of Boxing Day. The race was first organized in 1945 by the Tasmanian Yacht Club and is held over a route of just over 1,000 kilometres. The course is a notoriously hard one, usually held in poor weather conditions. Winning the event carries with it great prestige, as this is the major Australasian yachting race. The start, from Sydney harbour, is said to be one of the most beautiful of sights.

One of the best-known international racing events at sea is the one for the America's Cup. This is the cup won at the 1851 Isle of Wight race. It is called after the *America*, the vessel which won the race. It is a competition in which American vessels have usually triumphed.

One wealthy Irishman, Sir Thomas Lipton, was determined to wrest the trophy from the Americans. Between 1899 and 1930 he made five attempts to win the race, each time with a different sailing vessel named *Shamrock*. Lipton is said to have spent more than $15 million on his various challenges, but he never won the America's Cup. Other races which have caught the imagination of the public have been the single-handed competitions for yachting enthusiasts. In 1960, a competition was inaugurated for the first solo crossing of the Atlantic. The first winner was Francis Chichester, who was later knighted. In 1966-67 he also sailed single-handed round the world, in a ketch.

Handling a yacht in any weather conditions calls for a great deal of skill and much teamwork. At the start of a race the vessel has to hope to catch a good wind. Then the skill of the crew comes into play. The prevailing state of tides and currents will influence tactics and decisions will have to be taken about the amount of sail to be carried. Buoys and other course-marks have to be plotted and studied.

When other vessels are overtaken they have to be given plenty of room, so that they are not put in danger. Sometimes a vessel will capsize or go aground, and the crew will be called upon to take appropriate action to put things right.

81

Sailing vessels used for racing purposes are divided into two main classes – yachts and dinghies. There are also a number of minor categories. Yachts have decks extending along their length or part of their length. Dinghies were developed from the tenders which were kept once on the decks of larger yachts. They are small open boats capable of sailing in shallow water because of their wide bottoms.

In competitive events there are usually two crew members in a dinghy. They have to shift their weight from side to side as they manoeuvre their small craft in the wind. Both dinghies and yachts have sails. These are raised and lowered by ropes called 'halyards'. Another set of ropes, called 'sheets', control the sails once they have been raised.

The largest yachts used in in-shore races, i.e. events held close to the shore, are 12-metre ones. Those used for long-distance events may be considerably bigger. The size of a crew may vary, but the skipper is always very much in command.

Above: If they are properly taught, there is no reason why boys and girls should not take part in dinghy-racing like this. It is essential, however, that all children should learn to swim well before they take up sailing.

Right: These yachts are in full sail. If the vessels in a race are all the same size, there is no problem in deciding the winner – it is the first past the spot which has been designated as the winning-line (usually the place the race started). If yachts of different sizes take place in the same race, however, as is often the case, they are given handicaps in order to give every entry a chance. Time is added to the speed of the bigger, faster vessels.

Left: A catamaran in full sail. A catamaran has two identical hulls which are joined together across the deck. The water flows between the two hulls at a great rate as the wind catches the sail. Catamarans are spectacular in action, but are considered to be dangerous if they capsize, as they are difficult to right. A companion to the catamaran is the trimaran, which has three hulls.

Below: Canoe-racing at Fairfax harbour in Papua, New Guinea. Canoes are among the oldest of all sailing craft. Very long journeys have been made across the Pacific in them.

In addition to yachts and dinghies, there are a number of other vessels which have been used for speed sports, in competition with others or in races against the clock. The English Channel crossing, for example, has been tried by a number of different boats and ships. In 1885, the Oxford University rowing eight propelled their frail craft from Dover to Calais in 4 hours 20 minutes.

A more unusual crossing was made in 1911 by the Reverend Sidney Swann, who rowed across in a skiff, the lightest of rowing boats, in 20 hours. Before that, in 1911, Samuel Cody, an American who had made the first attempt to cross from France to England in a boat drawn along by a kite, succeeded in his aim.

One form of sailing is sand-yachting, in which a platform on wheels is driven by its sails along a beach. In 1956, four men on a sand yacht covered a mile (1.6 kilometres) in just over 62 seconds.

All who attempt to achieve great speeds hate to fail. At the 1976 Olympics, in one of the yachting events, a two-man British team finished 14th out of 16 entrants. Before coming ashore, they burnt their yacht!

Power-Boat Racing

Power-boats, craft propelled by engines either inboard or outboard, date back to 1887. Gottlieb Daimler, who developed the petrol-driven internal combustion engine, attached his invention to the stern of a rowing boat and drove it for a few metres across the River Seine. Two Britons, the Priestman brothers, built their own motor boat in the following year.

In an effort to encourage the growth of the new industry, an English newspaper owner, Sir Alfred Harmsworth, presented a trophy to be competed for by racing power boats. By the beginning of the 20th century the sport was already well-established. Small boat-races were being held all around the world – across lakes and other inland waterways.

As more powerful engines were perfected, off-shore races began to be held. Considerable speeds were reached on water, but designers were always worried about the dangers involved. There was always the chance of an engine developing a fault at high speed, while the force of the water could crush the hull of the craft. Over the years there were many fatal accidents, both in races and on high-speed record attempts. This did not deter enthusiasts. Races continued to attract many entrants.

For a long time one of the most popular was one held in the USA down the Hudson river from Albany to New York. Any type of boat was allowed to enter and dozens took part every year. In 1961, an annual power-boat race was instigated in Great Britain. It was routed from Cowes, in the Isle of Wight, to Torquay, some 322 kilometres. Later the course was doubled in length, entrants having to race from Cowes to Torquay and then back to Cowes again. Cowes week has become a very well-attended annual event.

Left: A Mexican speed-boat race takes place over rapids. Such boats are long and thin, with sharp bows to enable them to cut easily through the water. Drivers have to keep a sharp look-out for floating logs and other hazards.

Powerboat racing is divided into two main types, each equally spectacular. These types refer to the kind of engine being used – inboard or outboard. An inboard engine is situated inside the hull of the craft, while an outboard engine is attached to the exterior of the craft's hull. Within each of the two categories there are races for many different sizes of powerboat. Those propelled by inboard engines are capable of reaching speeds twice as fast as those driven by outboard engines.

There have been many famous powerboat racing drivers. One of the first was Garfield Wood, an American from Detroit. He won the Gold Cup four times between 1917 and 1921, and also broke the world record in a series of boats, each named *Miss America*. After this he won the international Harmsworth Trophy race on eight separate occasions in the 1920s and 1930s, causing the event to be abandoned for a time because he seemed to be unbeatable. One of Wood's

Right: As engines grew more powerful it became increasingly difficult to find suitable stretches of water over which to hold races. The rivers and lakes which once had contained dozens of craft at the massed starts of races could no longer provide enough space for the hydroplanes and other high-powered boats jostling for position at the beginning of events.

Below: Longer races began to be moved to more open stretches of water like the really big lakes and wide rivers, and then to off-shore courses. Races were held over longer distances, while fresh records were set for long-distance events for powerboats.

most unusual races was against an English woman, Miss Marion 'Betty' Carstairs, the winner of many important races in Europe. In 1930, she challenged Wood for the Harmsworth Trophy, but was defeated.

A great impetus was given to powerboat racing by the American designer, George F. Crouch. He built a powerboat with a hull which was V-shaped at the bottom, thus increasing the speed potential considerably. At first his design was banned by the authorities, who thought that such a craft was unsafe and would tip over at high speeds. Crouch proved that the authorities were mistaken. His concave-shaped hulls sold well and were adopted by boat-builders everywhere.

The next problem faced by designers was that the hulls of powerboats tended to cave in under the pressure of the water displaced as the boats sped through the water at their new increased speeds. Fresh materials were needed and these became available, first in the shape of plywood and then plastic. With the development of the jet engine the speeds reached by powerboats became even greater, bringing fresh problems to designers and organizers.

Water Records

Improvements in the design of powerboats led to greatly increased speeds in the pioneering days of powerboat racing. At first all craft were built with sharp bows in order to push their way through the water. Then designers tried in vain to invent engines which would be powerful enough to lift the hulls out of the water and thus skim along at even greater speeds. When this proved unsuccessful, they constructed flat-bottomed craft which would hurtle across the surface. Drivers soon began to establish new, much faster records.

Memorable records

Year	Name of powerboat	Driver	Speed (kph)
1903	*Napier*	Campbell Muir	40.1
1910	*Ursula*	Noel Robbins	70.2
1920	*Miss America*	Gar Wood	125.35
1930	*Miss England II*	Henry Segrave	158.94
1937	*Bluebird K3*	Malcolm Campbell	203.31
1950	*Slo-Mo-Shun IV*	Stan Sayres	258.01
1964	*Bluebird K7*	Donald Campbell	444.66
1978	*Spirit of Australia*	Ken Warby	510.46

Above: Donald Campbell crashes and dies in an attempt on the water speed record at Lake Coniston in 1967. His racing craft *Bluebird* turned over while travelling at great speed. Campbell, who had held the land speed record, was determined to hold the water speed title as well, like his father before him.

Left: Malcolm Campbell, the father of Donald, setting a new world record in an earlier *Bluebird* before the Second World War. Campbell was one of the greatest of powerboat drivers, who also set a number of land speed records after he left the Royal Flying Corps at the end of the First World War.

Right: The introduction of modern technology to attempts on land and speed records has led to the development of some remarkable engines, like this one by Ken Warby.

On the Water

Wherever there are huge waves, they always seem to attract surfers, who ride in on the breakers as they crash against the shore. Some athletes travel the world from beach to beach, seeking the perfect wave. Surfing is a sport with a long history. The first European visitors to the Pacific reported that the men of the islands regarded riding the huge waves as one of their favourite pastimes.

Today the best-known form of the sport is *long-board surfing*. In this the surfers rise to their feet on the boards, steady themselves and maintain their balance as they ride in. Skilled surfers are noted for the grace and the speed at which they can travel. Other forms of the sport include *body surfing*, in which the surfers lie horizontally without a board, and skim in to the beach; and *short-board surfing*, or *belly-surfing*, where the riders lie on their stomachs on the board.

All kinds of surfing are very popular in Australia and on the Californian coast of the USA, where surfers are always on the lookout for long, high breakers. Waves over ten metres high have been ridden by surfers. But the higher and faster the wave, the more difficult it is to control, especially if the wave rolls on for a long time as the surfer struggles to maintain his balance.

Above: Surfing is one of the most beautiful and spectacular of sports. Here a surfer in the Hawaiian islands is making a 'bottom turn'.

Left: Jet-skiing at San Diego, California, is a sport for the well-to-do.

Right: Windsurfing calls for dexterity and a sense of balance. The surfers have to balance on boards and catch a breeze in the sails. Then, they must be prepared to hang on as they are transported at great speed across the water.

Water-Skiing

A water-skier is towed over the water by a rope attached to the stern of a power-boat, while wearing two flat skis. The sport originated with the ski-tow races held in northern Europe, in which skiers were pulled over snow by teams of horses or single ponies.

The first national championships were held in the USA in 1939, and today world water-skiing championships are held every two years. The slalom events attract many entries. The course is 260 metres long and 23 metres wide. Six buoys have to be negotiated. Each time the skier is successful, the speed of his power-boat is increased by driving 3 kilometres an hour faster.

When a maximum speed of 58 kilometres an hour is reached, the length of the tow-rope is shortened after each successful run! A great deal depends upon the skill of the driver of the boat, who is a full partner in the event. Eventually, one person skies to victory.

Right: A competitor takes part in the 1981 world water-skiing championships. The wet-suit worn by a skier allows water to enter between the skin and the suit, but does not allow it out again. This water reaches the temperature of the body and keeps the skier warm.

Below: Bob la Point of the USA competes in the 1981 world championships. Skiers are towed up a ramp and leap as far as they can.

Index